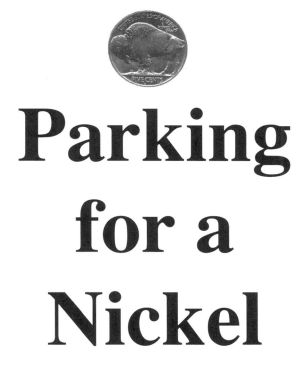

Parking
for a
Nickel

By Jack Fawcett

JCarp Publications, LLC

JCarp Publications, LLC
P.O. Box 130143
Ann Arbor, Michigan, 48113-0143
734-439-8031

Publisher's Cataloging-in-Publication
(Provided by Quality Books, Inc.)

Fawcett, Jack.
    Parking for a nickel / by Jack Fawcett.
    p. cm.
    Includes index.
    ISBN-13: 978-0-9758805-1-7
    ISBN-10: 0-9758805-1-9
    LCCN: 2005938585

    1. Fawcett, Jack. 2. Parking enforcement agents--
Michigan--Birmingham--Biography. 3. Birmingham (Mich.)
--Biography.   I. Title.

HE336.P37F39 2006   388.4'74'092
                             QBI06-378

Publisher's note: The majority of photographs are copied from old newspaper articles — many faded and yellow. Science and the editors have done their best to restore the photographs. Please forgive the poor quality and enjoy the journey into Jack's life.

Printed in the United States

ii

TABLE OF CONTENTS

Parking
for
a
Nickel

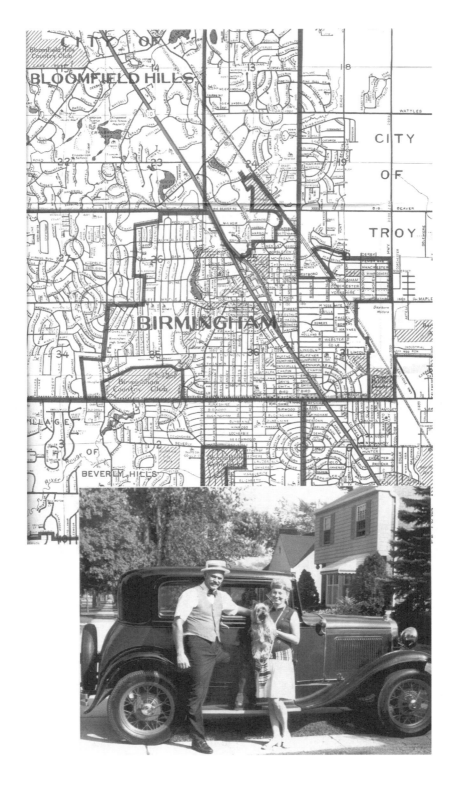

Prologue

Memories of a Parking Meter Man

All of my stories are true, even if some are over 50 years old. All of the characters are real. The names of some have been deliberately left out to protect the NOT so innocent.

I was hired by the City of Birmingham on March 1, 1947 as a water meter reader and repairman. After about 3 months, I was informed that I was to learn how to collect money from the parking meters. It seems that Hank Johns, the part time building superintendent and parking meter man, was going on vacation for 2 weeks. At the time there were about 250 meters in town and no parking lots. One day I was taken out to show me how to collect. The superintendent was named Hank and somewhat of a joker. He told me to watch out for a certain meter, but when I came to it I forgot and he didn't say anything. You had to hang on to the winding crank, after you wound up or the crank would unwind. It did and hit my knuckles about 50 times before I could get loose from it. Hank laughed so hard, he almost had an accident. My hand was numb for an hour. He said, "I told you to hang onto the crank." I said, "I know, but I forgot." I still remember and it has been 55 years.

In several of my stories you will find, that I have included my friend Al Sundell. He was the animal commissioner, as he liked to be called. We did quite a few capers together as you will see. We were good friends and still are. We went on many trips together, including our wives, of course. One trip was to England, Scotland and Wales. We rented a car and drove around for 3 weeks. It was one of the great times we all had.

When I started in 1947, the sign man and the dog catcher were repairing the parking meters. In May 1948, the city hired a firm of efficiency experts to go through every job and recommend changes to make things better. I was called in for my interview and was told that I was going to repair parking meters, besides water meters. I told the expert that I didn't know anything about parking meters. He said 'don't worry, we'll take care of that.' So for a week I drove to Ypsilanti, to a Park-O-Meter service center. After one week, I received a diploma that said I was fully trained to repair and service parking meters. By this time the city had added about 100 more meters. About this time in 1948, we got a new police chief. He had been a sergeant in Ypsilanti and was a great advocate of parking meters. I repaired parking meters for about 5 years. By this time we had 2 parking lots and many meters. A fellow with 30 years in the water meter department got the job to be a full time meter man. The city continued to add meters, until he retired in May 1958. By this time we had over 1400 meters. This meter man retired and I was appointed as parking meter supervisor in May 1958. I was sent to Jackson for a week at the parking meter service center. I stayed on this job for 25 years. My name is on a plaque on the Police Department's wall for 25 years service.

I forgot to mention that for 11 years, I set up voting machines for the elections in the city. After almost 11 years of setting up the voting machines, the city decided to send me to Jamestown, NY to the factory. This was a great trip and I had a great time. Three months later I was in the police department taking care of parking meters full time.

(Newspaper article)

BIRMINGHAM'S TOP METER MAN

All it takes is a turn of the screwdriver for Jack
Fawcett to fix those meters that stick

Life Among The Meters; Jack Fixes All For City

By Jass Thomas

      Innards of parking meters - dozens of them - most
ticking ominously, surround Jack Fawcett in his new
office-workshop in the Birmingham Police Station.

      Occasionally a "violation" flag drops in one of the
meters, but Jack is the one man in town who never has
to worry about putting in coins; he's Birmingham's top
meter man.

      In fact, he's solely responsible for the 1,248 one-
armed bandits standing around the sidewalks.

      A day in the life of a parking meter superintendent
can include such exotic problems as machines jammed
by foreign coins brought in by summer tourists, frozen

1

meters in the winter, bent coins all year 'round and spiders in the fall. Spiders?

"Yes," Jack explains, "spiders find the winder hole a handy place to crawl in to build a nest. Their webs go right across where the money drops and clog the meter....."

***

As a 1940 graduate of the then Baldwin High School, Jack remembers Birmingham before such contraptions as parking meters were dreamed of. With a name like Fawcett it was natural that his first job with the city was in the water department.

For more than 10 years he read and repaired that department's meters. At that time, too, he set up the area's voting machines. In 1958 the police department appointed the big, ruddy-faced man to his present job.

***

An extended beat opens this week for Fawcett and his two meter maids with completion of the $132,000 lot at Ferndale and Oakland. These additional 48 parking places, a welcome addition for Christmas shoppers, bring the total space in town to 2,900.   (Note: As of February, 2006, there are 1,270 parking meters and 3,579 parking spaces in downtown Birmingham bringing the total space to 4,849)

The $336,000 worth of coins Fawcett collects from them throughout the year in the trolley he's dubbed "Golden Goose" goes toward paying the $3 million owed for building Structure Number 1 at Oakland and N. Woodward and the new Ferndale-Oakland lot.

Would-be robbers should take note that the coin collector only has small amounts of money on him at any one time and that a Brink's armored truck collects the money he deposits at the treasurer's office.

***

High School sweetheart Shirley, whom Fawcett married 28 years ago, is secretary to Birmingham's city engineer. They have a house on Villa where he practices his hobby of photography.

While tinkering with one of the $60 meters, Fawcett recalled one irate woman's excuse when receiving a ticket for having a car parked at an expired meter: "Oh," she said, "I thought expired meant the meter was dead for the day."

Jack's redecorated workshop was once a jail cell. He points to a corner. "Two prisoners hung themselves over there about 25 years ago," he states. "But I don't think their ghosts will bother me any."

ABOUT THE AUTHOR

I was born on October 24, 1920, in Pontiac on Huron Street, just a block east of the Pontiac General Hospital. The hospital is still there but the name has been changed.

In 1925 we moved to Wing Lake. I went to Wing Lake School — a small one room school with outside plumbing. By the time I reached 6th grade there were too many students for one teacher, so for the 7th and 8th grades we were bused to Bloomfield Village School on Lasher, north of Maple. From there I went to old Baldwin High School on Chester and Maple in Birmingham. I graduated in 1940.

By this time I had I met my future wife, Shirley Shattuck. On October 1, 2005, we celebrated our 64th wedding anniversary.

My first job was as a carpenter's helper, which paid 50¢ an hour. I worked from 7 am to 5 pm, six days a week. After a few weeks the job was done. I then went to work for the wife of C.E. Wilson, who was the president of General Motors. They had a big estate on Long Lake Road on Island Lake. I mowed grass for about four days and did other odd jobs, like washing cars. They had eight cars — all GM, of course. Mrs. Wilson was a great lady to work for. This job was also a six days a week, nine hours a day. I had filled out an application at GM Truck in Pontiac several weeks before I was hired at the Wilsons. I received a letter asking me to come in to be interviewed. When I talked to the personnel man, he asked me if I really worked for the wife of the president of General Motors? When I told him I did, he then said, "When can you come to work?" I started at GM on October 1, 1940. They were making army trucks. Shirley and I were married one year later, and then came Pearl Harbor on December 7, 1941.

On March 23, 1943, I left Birmingham to join the U.S. Army. After 11 months of training, we took a voyage on the Queen Mary and landed in Scotland. We then took a slow train to the southern tip of England. I was in a 155mm artillery battery from Lansing — a Michigan National Guard outfit. I was classified as a lineman laying telephone wire and climbing poles.

We landed in Normandy about 10 days after D- Day. We fought our way through France, Holland,

Belgium and Germany. The Battle of the Bulge was the worst of the whole war.

We had to stop at the Elbe River to wait for the Russians to meet us. As the war ended we started doing occupation duty, which lasted about six months in Germany.

My mustering out rank was a technician 5th grade. I have five stars on my E.T.O. ribbon for five major battles. I also have a *Certificate of Merit* signed by the C.O. for the 119th Group. Only 10 of us received this honor.

I arrived back in Birmingham in November, 1945. I had been gone two years, seven months, and 14 days.

I signed up to go to school in Detroit at Electronics Institute, but after six months I quit and went to work for an apple farmer. But I knew the job would end in October.

I went to Pontiac Motors and filled out an application. The personnel man looked at it and said, "you're hired." I went to work that day for $1.25 per hour. I stayed there until February 1947.

I found out that the City of Birmingham was looking for someone to work in the water meter department. With a name like Fawcett, I just had to work in the water department. I applied and started work March 1, 1947. After 11 years of reading water meters, setting up voting machines, and repairing parking and water meters, the Chief of Police asked if I wanted to work for him. I did and he sent me to Jackson to train at the parking meter repair factory. After 4 days I returned to Birmingham to begin my new job where I stayed for 25 years.

If anyone goes in the Police Department, look on the east wall and you will see a plaque with my name on it as a retiree of the Police Department.

When I retired on January 3, 1983, the Birmingham Eccentric put my picture on the front page along with a pretty good story.

For a couple of years after I retired, a friend of mine, Herm Peters, and I painted garages. Then I became a volunteer for B.A.S.C.C., the senior center in Birmingham. I was asked to be a trustee for the foundation of Birmingham Senior Residents. Then as Baldwin House was built, my church, Embury Methodist, was one of the churches that built this senior residence. Our minister asked me to be on the board of directors.

I have been in the Birmingham Kiwanis Club for 45 years, serving as president three times. I belong to the Senior Men's Club of Birmingham. And, I enjoy playing golf.

Shirley and I have traveled extensively. We had two different motor homes and have been in all 50 States, Canada and Mexico. We have been to Europe four times from England to Greece and Turkey. We have also taken several Caribbean cruises. Our last trip was to Costa Rica where we spent 10 days. We have a manufactured home in a park in Bradenton, Florida.

I have six sisters — three who live near us when we winter in Florida, one in Alaska, one on Drummond Island and two in Waterford and one lives in Fenton, as well as a sister-in-law.

So, I have plenty of women to boss me around,

MY ANCESTORS

In the 1600s, a group of Fawcetts moved from England to Ireland as Quakers weren't exactly welcome in England. John and Judith Fawcett came from County Armogh, Ireland. They had one son, Thomas. He was married in 1708 and had four sons — Thomas, Richard, Joseph and John. The family of Quakers moved to Pennsylvania in 1736. In 1743 the Fawcetts moved to Virginia where each of the sons received 400 acres on the east side of Little North Mountain from Lord Fairfax. The original Fawcett homes were built here and the area became known as Fawcett Gap. As Quakers, the Fawcetts did not believe in slavery and eventually, a few of the families moved to Ohio near Xenia.

In 1862, my grandfather, John Lewis Fawcett, was born. He married Mary Thomas and they had 11 children — one of which was my father, Addison Fawcett, who was born in 1896. He married my mother, Lena Langdon, in 1919. I was born in 1920. My six sisters were to follow and they are all living. They have produced 21 nieces and nephews.

Shirley and I have no children, but as I told a newspaper reporter in Florida, "we're still trying."

a statement that made the front page the next day.

Although few Fawcetts live near the original Fawcett House in Virginia, the family name lives on. Housing developments are called Fawcett Gap Farm, Fawcett Run and Fawcett Lane. These facts were researched by my niece, Kerry Bennett, daughter of Nancy, who is proud to be a Fawcett and an eighth generation American.

THE LANGDONS
My mother's side of the family

The Langdons came from England in the late 1800s to Smiths Falls, Canada. My grandfather came to Canada about the same time. My Grandfather and grandmother met and were married and had one child. They moved to Orchard Lake, Michigan where my grandfather farmed on the island. They had six additional children. The farm house where the family lived for many years was on the spot that the Orchard Lake Country Club sits today.

My parents named me Jack Langdon Fawcett so I could carry on both names. I was named Jack after one of my mother's favorite uncles. In the 1920s he ran a boat livery on Orchard Lake where the State owned boat launch is located.

NORMANDY, FRANCE – JULY 1944

I was a telephone lineman in an artillery battery. We had 155mm rifles called Long Toms. We could shoot a 95 pound shell about eighteen miles. We had been in combat about thirty days and con- sidered ourselves veterans. We were fooled!! One bright sunny day, our bat- tery of 125 men and our four big guns had moved

into a small apple orchard. We placed our trucks and guns near the apple trees and strung our camouflage nets from the trees to cover our trucks. We hoped it would just look like trees. After my sidekick Mac and I had laid a couple miles of telephone lines, four of us decided to dig a four man fox hole. We dug it six feet wide, eleven feet long and four feet deep. We then liberated a wooden gate with wide boards on it, found some pipes to lay across the hole, then lay the gate on top of the hole. We put the sod back on top so it wouldn't look like a fox hole from the air. We then carried hay from a hay stack near us to sleep on as the dirt is kind of hard. Of course, we always slept with our clothes and shoes on. We slept toe to toe in the hole as we had two entrances. When it was almost dark we heard a plane coming. By this time we could tell a German plane. The motors made a different noise. Just before the German plane appeared, an ammunition train of eight GMC 6 x 6 trucks pulled into our field and tried to hide under the trees about hundred yards away. A German plane dropped about ten flares and lit the area up like day. We ducked in our fox hole. The dive bombers started dropping bombs and set some of the trucks on fire. The planes left and we came out of our hole to look around, until the shells on the trucks started exploding. About an hour later we heard the planes again. The planes again dropped more bombs as the trucks were still burning. The planes went away but returned after midnight to drop still more bombs. Some of those were about a hundred feet away. About this time there was a lot of praying going on in our fox hole. With two Catholics and two Protestants it must have worked as we didn't lose a man. A truck and the Captain's command car were damaged, and a couple of guys were buried but dug out. We found a few big steel splinters on top of our hole the next day.

We knew the Lord had been with us that night. This was one exciting night in the war and we had quite a few up until May 8, 1945. As they say, "There are no atheists in a fox hole."

ON TO GERMANY

My story of my WWII experiences focuses on just two days at Christmas time in 1944, in Germany. I was a PFC in the U.S. Army and a wireman/switchboard operator in a heavy artillery battalion. Wiremen were the soldiers who laid the phone lines for communication.

THE BATTLE OF THE BULGE

We were in the Battle of the Bulge in Germany near the Belgian border. Two of us had just laid a reel of wire for about a mile through very deep snow – perhaps 12-18 inches deep. It was extremely cold. Our unit had 155mm guns that could shoot for a distance of 18 miles. The shells for these guns weighed about 100 pounds and were six inches in diameter. We had just turned our guns toward the enemy's position.

Ten of us were stationed in a switchman's office building by the side of a railroad. Fortunately, it was made of brick but it only measured 12 x 15 feet. This is where we slept because it had a stove, and because the brick would ward off any shrapnel unless we happened to receive a direct hit.

CHRISTMAS DINNER WAITED OUTSIDE

About 150 feet past our building, eight Army trucks were lined up alongside the railroad tracks. These trucks were loaded with Christmas food – turkey with all the trimmings that could be provided in wartime. It was Christmas Eve, still and very cold. We were sitting inside, leaning against the walls and catching some sleep since it was so quiet. Piercing the quiet, one of our phones rang and we received a message from our fire direction center, telling us where to shoot at the enemy. I immediately phoned our gunners and shouted, "Fire mission," relaying the commands from our lieutenant. All four of our 155mm guns responded.

THE GERMANS BURNT OUR FOOD

Right after we fired, the Germans of course fired back. They hit all eight of our trucks, completely obliterating the turkeys and our Christmas meals. As a result, we ate beans out of cans on Christmas Day.

Despite the poor meal, it was a blessing that we did not receive a direct hit. The Germans evidently targeted the trucks, not the building. All 10 of us survived. We were certain that the Lord was in our little house with us on Christmas Eve, 1944.

Occupation duty in Germany — 1945

15

HUNTING WATER LEAKS

In 1948 I was in the water meter department for the City of Birmingham. The city had several wells at that time to pump water for everyone in the city. It was very hard water and you had to have a water softener or your sink or tub and stool would look like someone put rust in them. There were so many leaks in the water mains that the city figured they could only account for 46% of the water they pumped. We found some huge ones - you could have a large main leak under a paved street and it might never surface. It might run into a broken sewer and it would run for years. The City Manager at that time was Donald Egbert. He was an engineer, so he was determined to fix this problem. He bought an electronic leak detector. One day he came into the meter shop in the basement of City Hall. He told us about the leak detector and said, "If your guys find some good leaks, I'll give you a raise – if you don't, I'm going to kick some ass." I still remember this speech of his and it's been over fifty years. We, Gene Hemmerly and I, worked hard at finding leaks and found some real big ones. We did get a good raise as this was before unions. Gene and I worked good together. We had gone to grade school and high school together. Also we had both worked at the same GMC truck plant in Pontiac after high school. Then he married Thelma Mason, a gal I had known since she was three years old. She lived across the street from me for about sixteen years and was my wife's maid of honor when we got married.

Back to looking for leaks. We started a program about April 1st to check all hydrants in the city with the leak detector. It had a microphone on twenty feet of wire, so we could leave the instrument in the truck and just pull the wire over to where the hydrant was. If there was water running in the block the mike would pick up the noise. The electronic box was like a radio I guess. Sometimes we would pick up radio programs. Once I remember we picked up "Ma Perkins", a soap on the radio. After we had checked all the hydrants in town – the ones we had heard water running – we started checking each house in the block. All dwellings have a shutoff valve at the street which is usually four feet below the sidewalk on the waterline. We had a solid pipe with a slot on one end to turn the valve off or on. If you don't pay your bill, this is where they shut off your water. Sometimes as we put the key down on the valve we could hear on the ear phones people talking in the house. Once I remember one lady was really giving her husband holy hell. This was really interesting work and I enjoyed it very much. We never told anyone which houses the people were fighting or swearing in. Sometimes I knew the people in the house, but never told them.

The 1960s

STOLEN CAR

One morning as I started collecting in Lot 1 — now Deck 1 at Pierce and Merrill — a car was parked with the motor running. I looked inside to see if someone was sleeping. It was empty and no keys were in the ignition. It looked kind of weird so I went into the police department and reported it. I gave them the license number. An officer checked the number and found it had been stolen the night before in Royal Oak. The car was running because it had been hot wired. Whoever stole it just parked it and walked away. The police towed it to the pound.

THE THIEF

One day, just before 5:00, which was quitting time, then Chief Moxley called me to his office. He asked me if the sign man's helper was collecting for me. I told him no. The chief had been on the top floor of the Wabeek Building at a doctor's office. He heard a noise that sounded like coins dropping in a tin can. As he looked out the window, he saw the sign man's helper collecting money on Bates Street. He had a

19

two quart tin can. The chief asked me to go over on
Bates and check to see if the meters were empty. I
checked all the meters on the west side. All eight
were empty and I returned and told the chief what I
had found. He said don't tell anyone, I'll take care of
it tomorrow. The next day this helper and the chief
drove past me as I was collecting by the library. Later
in the day Chief Moxley called me to his office. He
explained the helper had confessed to stealing $80.00
and had paid it back. He was then allowed to resign.
I told the chief that this kid was going to school to
be a lawyer. The chief said, "he should be a good
one, he's crooked enough." This kid got off work
at 4:30 and came up town to make a little money.
The sign man kept a set of meter keys in his truck
glove compartment. He had to change meter heads
occasionally, as some posts were loose or damaged.
In the next few days, while collecting, I found quite
a few more meters that were short of money. He had
probably collected a lot more than he had confessed
to. From then on, the keys were kept locked in the
Treasurer's vault each night. We never had that kind
of problem from employees again. Also, the sign man
never got to carry keys in the glove compartment.

If he needed to remove a meter, he came to me and I unlocked it for him. It took more time, but it was safer.

GOOFY LADY

One day when I was in the police department, a lady came in waving a ticket. The desk sergeant didn't like to argue with citizens about tickets, especially women. He asked me to take care of the lady. She was very excited and unhappy. She said, "I don't deserve a ticket." I asked her what kind of coins she had put in the meter. She replied, "Coins? I didn't put any coins in. The red flag said expired and I thought it meant it was dead for the day."

I took her in to see my supervisor Lt. Thomason, then left quickly.

True story.

SKUNK STORY

Some afternoons I would go to coffee with Al Sundell, the dog warden. One day he asked me to go to the dog pound in his pick up. Afterward, we would stop at the Whistle Stop for coffee. It was a very hot day in July. As we went east on Maple, the light at Woodward turned red. Al stopped quickly and the street was rough there. The truck sort of shuddered and as he had three young skunks in a cage in the back, they all cut loose their odor. It covered the intersection like a blanket. People were shaking their heads and looking around. It was so strong, you couldn't breathe. All we could do was laugh and wait for the light to change.

We called this a real gasser.

FEMALE DENTIST STORY

On North Woodward, close to where Carrie Lee's Chinese Restaurant was, there was a female dentist. She was German and a real bitch. She insisted on parking right in front of her office. Now these were two hour meters and you were supposed to move after two hours. I overlooked her a lot as she came out swearing at me if I was writing her a ticket. There were twelve hour meters across the street, but she chose not to use them. I told her one day that if she parked across the street she probably wouldn't get any more tickets. She swore at me and said she would park any place she wanted to. I told her that my boss, Lt. Thomason, said to tell her if she was getting too many tickets or not enough, to call him. She said, "You are a son of a b@*#^, and so is your boss." Upon hearing this he said, "Don't show her any mercy." I didn't and she soon moved out to Lahser and Maple. As she was next door to my dentist, I saw her car parked in the alley. I went to my dentist one day. On the way out I placed an empty violations envelope on her windshield. This was to let her know I had not forgotten her. I bet the air was blue when she went home. But in a small way, I got some revenge.

ANNIE SMITH

This story could be called my most unforgettable character. Annie was a local character who annoyed many people in City Hall and elsewhere. I kind of liked her, as she would say anything to anybody at any time. She used colorful language part of the time. If she didn't like someone, she told them in no uncertain terms. She was about 75 and acted like she was one brick short of a load. But she was no dummy! This happened the time Ronald Reagan came to speak at Shain Park when he was running for president. Just before he spoke, I left City Hall by the rear door to go collect at lot 7 near the community house. As I got to Henrietta Street, a small man in a dark suit came up to me, flipped a leather case at me and said, "Secret Service." He said, "Do you know a lady named Annie Smith?" I replied I did. He wanted to know if I knew where she was. I said, "She is right over there on the corner looking at you." I said, "Come on, I'll introduce you to her." I said, "Annie, this gentleman is Secret Service." She said, "What do you want?" He said, "Could I look in your purse?" Now her purse was a coal scuttle. She wore high shoes, long dresses and wide brimmed hats. He blinked a couple of times, examined her purse, said thanks and walked away. Annie said, "What the hell did he want?" I was surprised that she didn't explode on him. She was on the Secret Service list of kooks. Actually she just spoke her mind and if some cuss words came out, so much the better. When she parked at a meter, she usually put a rag or paper bag over the meter. I would take the rag off the meter and put one hour on the meter. This was easier than listening to her excuses. I never gave her a ticket. Like me, she was always friendly. Right after I retired, I was out at Kmart one day. I heard a voice hollering, "Jack Ass,

Jack Ass." I knew it was Annie. I sat and had coffee with her so she would be quiet. She died quite a few years ago, but is the most unforgettable character I've known.

THE LINEUP

Working in the Police Department was a real adventure. Some of the police officers were characters. One is a detective I won't name. He had me get in quite a few lineups where someone would look through a two-way mirror at a line up of five to six people. Several times it was some guy who exposed himself. One day I got in a lineup with five other guys. I found out later two were bank robbers. They had cuts on their faces from flying glass when the police shot out the windows on their car. Luckily they were identified by several people. Most of the times the detective would say "Go in there and get in the lineup." I always did it just to help them out. This was my last lineup. One day as I came in the police department, the detective said, "Quick, go in that room and get in the lineup." I asked what it was for and he said, "Just go on in." I looked the five over and decided that one was guilty of something.

He was a little guy about 50 years old in a suit. He looked kind of shifty so I thought he was guilty of something. We heard some ladies giggling in the next room as they looked through the mirror. Soon the detective opened the door and said, "You can all go, but Jack, you stay." He was laughing as I said, "Did they pick the right guy?" He said yes. I asked who it was and he said, "You!" I didn't think it was very funny, but he did. But this is not the end of this story. A week later as I collected in lot 6 behind the Reid Building, some of the people on the third floor opened the window and hollered "Hi, Swinger." This was repeated every time I went in the parking lot to repair a meter or collect. The people were dentists, doctors, and nurses. I just laughed and waved back. By asking a friend of mine, who was a postman, he told me that at the last meeting of the Metropolitan Club, made up of policeman who knew all about it, postmen and firemen everybody found out that I was picked as the exposer. Actually, the guilty guy was a psychiatrist, but without any identification he went free. I guess the women who were playing golf weren't looking at his face. I was called "Swinger" for several months and by one mailman for years.

    End of that story!

FIDO ESCAPADE

One year in November, I went for coffee with Al, the dog warden. As we left City Hall, he got a call that a dog had broken through the ice on Quarton Lake. We drove down there in a hurry and sure enough, a black dog was trying to get out of a hole in the ice. The ice wasn't strong enough to hold us to walk on. The dog was very tired and didn't look like he would last long. The only person that had a boat lived on the other side of the lake. He was Marshall Fredericks on Lake Park Street. We drove over there very fast and explained to Mrs. Fredericks our need for a boat. She said, "Take ours." We ran down the hill and had to break the ice to get the boat in the water. Al stood in the front breaking ice and I paddled in the rear. It took awhile to get across the lake, but we finally made it. The dog was about a block up the lake. We still had to get the boat up there. There was about four inches of snow, so we got on each side of the boat and ran sliding the boat on the snow. It was tough going, but we got there and broke the ice, as the dog was about 50 feet out in the lake. He started to go down as we got there, but Al grabbed his collar and hauled him in the boat. As we got to shore, the dog jumped on land and ran like somebody was after him. He never said thanks or looked back. I guess he headed for home. We were really tired but happy we had saved his life. Sometimes when I went with Al for coffee, I got more than I bargained for as you can tell from some of my stories. I still talk to Al on the phone and see him once in awhile.

HIPPY GIRL

This story is about a meter in lot 2. This is where the parking deck at Ferndale and Oakland is located. This lot had about 200 meters in it, some two hours, some four hours, some twelve hours. One morning while collecting I came across a jammed meter. It had a key jammed in it. This happened once in awhile, as some people tried to get time this way. I pried the key out and threw it out into Oakland Avenue. I finished collecting and went back to City Hall. About 4:00 in the afternoon, a call came into the police department from a gal who said she worked at Demerys. She had stuck her switch key in the meter in the morning and now it was gone. I let her stew for a while and finally drove over there. A gal was sitting in her car. She said her key had been stuck in the meter and without it she couldn't start her car. I questioned her about the situation then told her I had thrown the key out into Oakland Avenue. I walked out where I had thrown the key in the street and there it was. It had been there all day. I took it back to her and she got in her car. As I started to walk away, she said, "You're weird sir." No thanks or anything. I replied, "I may be weird but I don't stick my keys in parking meters. Next time I'll throw it down the sewer."

No problems with her ever again.

THE $500.00 GIRL

One day the chief called me into his office and said, "Do you know this person?" It seems that she owed $500.00 in parking tickets. I said I did and that I had written a couple of dozen of those tickets. She worked uptown near Huston Hardware. The chief said take an officer over and arrest her. I had to remind the chief that I was a civilian. He called the Sgt. and said, "Get Jack an officer to go arrest a gal uptown for nonpayment of parking tickets." We went over, the officer arrested her and took her to the station. She was then taken upstairs to the courtroom.

This was about 10:00 am. The judge asked her if she could pay her tickets and she said no. He said he'd give her until 4:30 that afternoon or she might spend the next few days in the county jail. At 4:25 pm, she came in and paid the $500.00 in cash. I told her to park in the lot behind Demerys.

We never saw her again or her car.

WRESTLING MATCH

In 1963 I was elected president of the Birmingham Kiwanis Club. We were always looking for ways to make money to send kids to camp, give scholarships and baskets of food at Christmas time. One of our members, Al Thomas, was a referee for

big time wrestling on TV. Through him we got some big time wrestlers to sign on. They agreed to do it for free as they knew the money would go for kids or charity.   This picture shown above was the signing of "Leaping Larry Shane", a real character. The other person, on the far left, is Chuck Mosher. Larry borrowed my watch for the picture then didn't want to give it back. We had the match at Groves High School. We sold tickets for two weeks before the wrestling match. It was a huge success. The night of the match our Kiwanis members were ushers and ticket takers. As a treat, the wrestlers brought two midgets to wrestle. One midget was named "Happy Humphrey" and wrestled another midget. He also put on a real show by hitting the two big guys in the knee then running under the ring. The crowd seemed to enjoy the show and our Kiwanis club enjoyed the couple thousand we made.

Anyway this is my story about our wrestling match. It paid off pretty good, but we never tried it again.

I have been a member of the Birmingham Kiwanis for forty-six years and have been president for three terms.

"GOLDEN OLDIE" (October, 2005)

I belong to the Senior Men's Club of Birmingham. We are allowed 450 active members. We meet on Fridays from 10:30 until 12:00. Then we have a lunch if you want it. We have committee reports first, then our program. Usually a speaker and the programs are very good. We meet in the Birmingham Community House. The program on October 14th was Congressman Joe Knollenberg. This is the day I was inducted as a "golden oldie". You have to be 85 years old and been in the club for 10 years. At this time I also became a life member. We had 299 members in attendance on Friday. In the club are some fellows I went to high school with in Birmingham. Also several are from the church I attend. Several more are from the Kiwanis Club I belong to. Some I know from working for the City of Birmingham for 36 years. One fellow is my former boss, retired City Manager Bob Kenning, a friend and neighbor.

The fellow in the picture with me is John Crawford.

He is a long time friend. I got him to join the Kiwanis Club about 30 years ago. Also we have played many games of golf together. I had the pleasure of inducting him into the Senior Men's Club just two weeks ago. If you become an applicant you will probably wait for close to three years before you can be a member. I waited almost five years before being inducted. It is really a great bunch of senior men and I enjoy attending very much. A few years ago I met a fellow who was in the Army with me in 1943, George Cleland. I hadn't seen him since then. My father-in-law was a charter member of this club. His name was Arthur Shattuck.

The 1970s

HOW I STARTED WRITING TICKETS

In 1972, we got a new chief of police, Roland Tobin. He called me into his office one day and said, "Jack, I'm going to have you write parking tickets." I said, "I don't know about that." He said, "What do you mean?" I said, "Well, I'm a civilian and it may not be legal." He replied, "By God, we'll make it legal." I followed him up to the city attorney's office.

He told the attorney what he wanted. The attorney looked through the huge book of city ordinances and said, "Write 'em." So one of the meter maids showed me how to write a ticket. I even remember the first ticket I wrote and where. It was what now is in front of the Townsend Hotel. A gal that worked in a beauty parlor was my first victim. She was always parked at an expired meter. Just 50 feet away was a 150 meter parking lot. I got her many more times during the next year. There was a stockbroker firm, also nearby on Townsend. A gal, Jane, was a broker. One day, the Chief said, "She owes $200.00. Do you know her and where she works?" I told him I did and would talk to her. I knew the manager of the firm so I went to his office and told him about it. I could see he was not pleased. About an hour later, she came in to City Hall and paid all her tickets. She never got another ticket. The Chief gave me many little jobs like this. The first month I wrote about 300 tickets thinking the Chief would say slow down. He called me in and said, "I love it." I said, "How about a raise if you like it so much?" He replied he couldn't as I belonged to the *Teamsters*.

CASE OF THE DISAPPEARING MONEY

This story took place in the early 1970s. One day, as I was collecting on Bates near the library, I came upon several meters with no money. It was shortly after 8 am and no cars were parked there yet. I checked to see if they were running and they were okay. Going down Merrill, I ran into the same problem. Most meters were empty or had a few nickels in them. As I went down South Woodward, I had the same problem. Later in the day I checked further down South Woodward as far as Frank. The same problem — not much money. I figured out that somebody had a key and was collecting at night. I let my supervisor know what I had found and what I believed. The meters being emptied all had the same key number. We had about 500 meters with the same key number. Lt. Thomason put out an order for the midnight shift to watch at Bates and Merrill for anyone unlocking meters. After three nights they hadn't seen anyone, but the money kept disappearing. One officer told me they saw a guy on a bicycle at 3 am. ride past with a handbag on the handlebars. I think this was the guy responsible for the theft. Lt. Thomason asked me what we should do. I told him the meters being robbed are all #50 locks. If we bought new locks at $10.00, it is a lot of money. We knew we had to change locks to stop this character from stealing more money. I called the parking meter supervisor in Pontiac and told him our problem. He said he had a bucket full of locks from meters they had removed or junked. He said I could use them and bring back the ones we exchanged. I went up there and got the locks. I started exchanging locks at nights after 5 pm and worked until 8:00. After four days it was Saturday. I worked 10 hours on Saturday and some nights the next week. After changing the locks the collections increased right away. They never caught the culprit, but I had some suspicions as the midnight collections started right outside the post office and ended up by 555 South Woodward. I took the 500 locks back to Pontiac and thanked them very much. As this story ended, we never knew how someone got a key. It wasn't one of ours. I had saved the city thousands of dollars for a few hours of overtime.

THE BINGO CHIP CAPER

One day as I collected up on North Woodward, I noticed bingo chips in several meters. I only collected these meters once a week on Wednesday. Over the next few weeks I kept finding bingo chips in the meters. They were red, white, and blue — very patriotic but not legal. They were the size of quarters. At 25¢ per chip, it soon ran into a lot of money. I started saving them so that whoever was doing it couldn't use them over. I soon had a large assortment of red, white and blue chips. I tried to see which car it was, but it was always a different one. This went on for several weeks, so I decided to catch the culprit. I went to work at 6:00 am one day and sat up on the hill on Harmon Street. I had collected all the money out of the meters on the west side of Woodward. From the hill on Harmon it was about 200 yards to Woodward. It is a small hill and I had the department field glasses. At about 7:45 am, a car pulled up at a meter across from a dentist's office. A young lady got out and put some coins in the meter. Her back was towards me so I couldn't see the meter. After she went into the dentist's office, I went up to the meter and checked it. Two pennies were showing in the two coin windows. It took no pennies. Upon opening the coin box, I found a bunch of red and blue bingo chips. I now knew who it was. She would put bingo chips in, then two pennies to push the chips down to the coin box so I wouldn't see them. The meters took nickels, dimes and quarters — no pennies. I waited a couple of hours then took a handful of chips and went into the dentist office. I went up to the receptionist and said, "Look what I found in your meter." She smiled and said, "Yes, I only do it when I'm broke and today I am broke." I went to the Detective's office and told my story to the Detective Lieutenant. After hearing my story and showing the bingo chips to him, he told a detective to go arrest her. I went with him to identify the culprit. The detective told her she was under arrest and we took her to the police station. She was fingerprinted and photographed and taken up to see the judge. She was arraigned and wanted a trial, as she pleaded not guilty. A court date was set in 48th District Court in two weeks. She didn't use any bingo chips while awaiting trial, although she was at work each day. When we went to court, she had a lawyer who I thought was an ass. He asked me some foolish questions and right away I knew he knew nothing about parking meters. Our city attorney wasn't much better. He asked me why it took so long to catch her. I had found that she kept changing cars and parked at several different meters. They were there for 12 hours and she would stay all day. Also, some days she used real money. After about 20 minutes of testimony on my part, she didn't take the stand. The judge went out in the hall for about five minutes. When he returned he asked the defendant's attorney if he could ask me a question. The judge then asked me if I had mentioned pennies when I went into the dentist's office to confront her. She must have told her attorney that she put pennies in to push the bingo chips down in the coin box. The judge said, "I find you guilty. $200.00 court costs, pay all your tickets today, on probation for one year, any more tickets and I will frown on it."

CITIZEN COMMENDATION

Chief Tobin was a real good guy to work for. He told me if I had any trouble with anyone to come and see him. I did a couple of times and the trouble disappeared. He had been a Sergeant in the Detroit Police Department and also State Police. He was really street smart. One day on my lunch hour, I was uptown and walking by Detroit Bank & Trust, now Comerica. This was June 11, 1975. A gal I knew told me that a gypsy standing over by the bank, was trying to pull something funny. She had an envelope full of money and said she had found it. If my friend would give her some money to show her good faith, she would share. I knew where the gypsy lived, in a big house on North Woodward, north of Oakland, now gone. I went to the Police Department, told Chief Tobin about the problem. He had me take an unmarked car to watch the house. The detectives showed up and raided the house with a search warrant. The gypsy lady was there and admitted to trying the pigeon-drop scheme. Her husband had escaped and was not around. His new Chevrolet was impounded. It turned out that he had bought a Cadillac on a scam in Pennsylvania and traded it for a Chevrolet in Detroit. He was a well-known scam artist. A few weeks later he was caught and prosecuted. One Monday night, I was asked to come to the city commission meeting. The mayor presented me with a Citizen Commendation. It is framed and on the wall of my family room. The gal who tipped me to the scam also got a commendation.

The commendation I received says that I helped recover $3,000.00.

There must be some pigeons in Birmingham.

CAKE STORY

One day we went to the Whistle Stop for coffee. The owner, Catherine Griffith, asked how the Chief's secretary, Winnie Singers, was. Al said, "She is okay. Today's her birthday." Catherine said, "I'll send her a piece of cake." She cut a huge piece of cake and we took it and left. About two blocks away I said, "Pull over to the curb, Al." He said, "What do you have in mind?" I said, "If we take this cake back to the Police Department, those cops will eat it." So we cut it in two pieces and ate it. About a week later, Catherine came to city hall to pay her water bill. I was in the hall and heard Catherine ask Winnie how she liked the cake she sent for her birthday. Winnie replied, "My birthday is next October. This is July."

Catherine opened her eyes real wide and said, "Damn those guys."

IRATE CUSTOMER

On North Old Woodward, there are some small stores across from Harmon. One business owner was a real pain in the you know what. He racked up many tickets, as he wanted to park almost at his door. As usual, across the street were all day meters, same price, he just didn't want to bother. One day, the chief said go see this guy. He owes over $200. I tried to talk to him, but he blew up and ordered me out of his store. I called Lt. Thomason on the jeep radio and he said he would send "the hook". That's what we called Bob Adams' wrecker. I told him to send a police officer also as this guy is trouble. The police officer arrived in five minutes. I told him the situation and that the guy was going to be trouble. He was pretty big and said don't worry. I'll take care of it. The wrecker arrived and hooked onto the rear end of the car and lifted it up. At this time the guy who owned the car came charging out. He was really upset and was swearing. He asked what was going on. The police officer said, "We're impounding your car for nonpayment of your parking tickets." The guy then said, "You can't do this" and hit the officer in the chest with both hands, pushing him over the hood of the police car. The police officer then grabbed the guy, threw him to the street, turned him over and put a knee in his back. Then he handcuffed him and pushed him into the back of the police car. At this time I was glad the officer was there. The guy was taken to the police department, booked and put in the pokey (jail). Later he was taken before the judge. He pleaded guilty, as witnesses, including myself, testified to his behavior. He was fined big time, paid his tickets, warned by the judge with jail time if he didn't straighten up. In one month he moved to Royal Oak.

Good riddance.

SWAN SONG

This was in November, 1977. It was getting cold and time to get the swans off Quarton Lake. There were three — two white, one black. This day, Al found they had crossed under the Oak Street bridge and were in a swampy place north of there. He asked me if I would help him catch them. I said okay. I had never caught a swan or touched one. I chased a white one and he or she ran into a bush and was stuck. I pulled him or her out, held its head with one hand and held its body with the other. It then had a bowel movement like none I've ever seen. It was black like muck and smelled like dead fish. It ran down my arm into my hand and out between my fingers. It also ran down my jacket and pants. It really smelled. Al laughed so hard I thought he would have an accident. We took the swans out to the dog pound where a special pen had been built for them for the winter. I thought this was beyond the call of duty.

BIRTH CONTROL PILLS

One day in the winter when the snow was about 10 inches deep, Chief Tobin asked me to go to some businesses on South Woodward and have them clean their sidewalks. I told him I had no authority to do this. He said if anyone gives you a hard time tell them you are acting under my orders and either they do it by 5 pm or get a ticket. He said he'd back me up on anything. My first target was the Chrysler dealer at Woodward and Grant. His used car lot had been cleaned and the snow pushed on the Frank Street sidewalk. It was about three feet deep and impossible to walk on. I told the manager and he wasn't happy. I told him if he didn't clean it up in one hour, the Chief himself would be down to see him and he wouldn't be happy. They soon had a jeep with a snowplow to clean it off. I inspected it and told the Chief it was okay. Next was a couple of businesses on Woodward near uptown. They complied right away. The Chief said I had done a good job. About 1977, we got a new Chief of Police. He was a lieutenant in the police department, so we all knew him. He was very good to work with also. I was writing about 3000 tickets a year and some I had to go to court on. The Chief kept track of various places that workers were parking at meters all day in violation of our parking ordinance. Merchants would call him and tell him which block this occurred in. He would call me in and give me a certain location to mark tires. Now this was a meter maid's job, but he thought I would do a better job. I did. I would mark a tire with blue chalk. Sometimes certain people would come out with a cloth and wipe it off. They wanted to park in front of the store or office that they worked in. My job was to discourage this practice. When I found a car or cars I thought were trying to fool me, I would place an object on top of the tire in the tread, also marking the tire down below. When I came back and the blue mark was gone but the object I placed on top of the tire was still there, they got a ticket. Now these tickets weren't overtime at a meter. They were prohibited overtime tickets. The fine was more than doubled, so it cured an awful lot of unlawful practices. Once I found a box of birth control pills. I kept them to put on the top of the tire. One of my customers got about seven of these expensive tickets and hired a lawyer. When I went to court, I explained on the witness stand how I marked the tire, but not about the pills on the top of the tire. The Judge was Alice Gilbert, who I thought was a fair Judge. I had to read one ticket and I had left my glasses in the workshop. The gal's lawyer kept picking at me saying, "He can't even read the ticket." I could, but slow. The Judge said, "Just let him alone, he's doing OK." Finally when all my testimony was finished, the judge said to me, "How do you know she wiped off the blue chalk?" I told her I didn't want to tell everybody my secrets. Judge Gilbert said, "This time I think you better." So I told about putting the birth control pills in the tire tread. Everyone in the courtroom laughed. The Judge smiled. She also pointed to the defendant and said, "You are guilty. $200.00 fine, pay all tickets, court costs, and probation with no tickets for one year."

I never saw this lady or her car again.

HARVEY KRESGE

This was in the 1970s. One day while in Kresge's store, at Henrietta and Maple, I met a guy who the waitress behind the food counter introduced as Harvey Kresge. He was the new store manager. Some of us at City Hall went there for coffee breaks sometimes. We talked to him and he seemed like an average guy. He soon let me know he was from the Kresge family. He also told me he didn't like paying to park at his own store, especially as he was the manager. There were 26 meters in the little lot behind the store. I told him I couldn't help him, but he might get the City Commission to listen to him, seeing as he was a Kresge. He went to the Commission meeting one night and stated his case. The result was I had to remove one meter next to the far building. A sign was put up saying, *No Parking, Manager*. This pleased him to no end. I used to see him after he left as manager. He would walk around town and would see me collecting. He was a real nice man. He died recently. They took the meters out a few years ago — the city took it over for some city cars.

ALLIGATOR STORY

One day in the summer of 1975, Al Sundell, the animal commissioner, got a call that an alligator was chasing four ladies in the backyard on Hanna Street. He asked if I could give him a hand. I decided that the ladies had been sipping the hard stuff, so I said sure. When we arrived, the alligator was running around the backyard. He was about three feet long and quite aggressive. I guess he was hungry. I told Al that I'd hold the door open for him. He had a van with a big cage in the rear to put dogs in. Al caught him by the tail and swung him into the cage. I shut the door and we had him. Al took him to Jungle Jims in Royal Oak.

A year later, we found out where he came from. It seems a kid brought him back from Florida and kept him in a cage in the garage. But it kept growing and getting pretty hungry, so it dug its way out and canvassed the neighborhood for food. He was pretty big when we caught him. He surely scared all the neighbors.

FOXY FAWCETT

This story is about a lady who worked for a

business on old North Woodward, about five stores south of Carrie Lee's Chinese Restaurant. She drove a purple Gremlin. This fact alone should alert you to the kind of person she was. She was a secretary in a stockbroker business. She wanted to park in front of this business. There were two hour meters and the same old story of not wanting to park across the street at all day meters. I was asked by the chief if I could discourage the practice. I drove a three wheel Cushman cycle up there sometimes to ticket the purple car. She would hear me coming and run out and put money in the meter. So to beat her, I would park about 10 or 12 cars away and walk close to the buildings while writing the ticket. I had the license number in my little black book that I kept for special folks. I would walk up and put the ticket in her windshield before she could run out and put money in. This really annoyed her. I told her to park across the street but she said she could park anywhere she wanted to. I told her to save her money, as she would need it to pay her tickets. She wrote a letter to my supervisor, Lt. Squire, and accused me of skulking up the street. She called me Foxy Fawcett and said I was a gossip. Lt. Squire called me in and gave me the letter. I have it yet today. He asked me if I was a gossip. I replied sure. "Is it against the law?" He said no. I found out later one meter maid was her friend and told her when I would be looking for her car. I told this meter maid to stop this B.S. or she'd be looking for another job when I told the chief. She quit soon after that, as she was pregnant.

Served her right.

One thing I always said was, anybody who drove a purple Gremlin would sleep in their underwear.

THE BELL CAPER

Over by what is now the Baldwin House, there was an access drive on Chester Street. We had twelve 12 hour meters there for people who worked all day. I only collected these meters one day a week, on Mondays. One Monday I found no coins in the end meter towards Martin Street. I put it in my book, came back later and checked the timer. It seemed okay, so left it until the next Monday. This time it also had no money. I knew something was wrong. I told my supervisor, Lt. Thomason, that I would like to come in early the next morning, as I wanted to go fishing.

He said okay so I came in at 6:00 the next morning. I collected all the money out of these 12 meters so I could tell what was going on. I had the police field glasses - very strong. You could see a pimple on a flea's behind at 50 yards. I parked in St. James Church lot on Martin, so I was closer than 100 yards away. At 7:00 a car pulled up to the end meter. A person pulled something out of his pocket and inserted it in the meter. He pushed it in and out about two times. As he walked near my car I shielded my face so he couldn't see me, as I knew who he was. He worked at Bell Telephone on the corner across from City Hall. I knew his name, so when Lt. Thomason came to work at 8:00 am I was waiting for him. He said, "Did you have any luck fishing?" I told him what I had caught and the guy's name and where he worked. I should have been a detective. We went to see Chief Tobin and told him the story. He called Bell security in Detroit. Two hours later, Charlie walked in and gave himself up. When asked what he was using, he showed us a flat piece of plastic cut at an angle. It worked just as if you put quarters in. He admitted that his girlfriend did the same thing. I quickly retired about 25 old meters. The city didn't prosecute and that ended the story.

Oh yes, Charlie never talked to me again.

I wonder why?

BICYCLE CAPER

One day Al Sundell and I went to see Chief
Tobin to see if we could get a bicycle at the upcoming
auction. We told him we knew of a foster boy in town
who had his bike stolen. He said do what you have
to do to get the boy a bike. We would have to bid on
a bicycle, deciding to keep it legal. We picked a real
nice bike from the collection in the police department.
We took it down to my workshop in the city hall
basement. We took off the wheels, handlebars and
seat. With just the frame we figured we could get it
cheap. It turned out I got the bid for $2.00. This was
Saturday. On Monday we put it back together and
took it down to the boy. He was so happy that he had
tears in his eyes. We did also. We went in to tell the
chief about it. Before we could tell him, he asked,
"Did you get the boy a bike?" We said yes and started
to tell him about it. He said, "Don't tell me, I don't
want to know. Do you need money?" We said no, we
had taken care of it. He said, "Good job. Now go get

coffee." We felt pretty happy about the deed, even if it was just a little "shady".

We felt it was almost legal.

RED MUSTANG STORY

This took place in lot 4, a metered lot now a deck across from Peabody's. I collected there Mondays and Thursdays. One Thursday morning about 10:00, I collected there and gave a ticket to a red Mustang. It had no front license plate, which at that time you had to have. In the afternoon I came back to fix a meter and found the red Mustang still there at an expired meter. This was a 2-hour meter, so legally I could have written a ticket every two hours. It was still there, so I gave it another ticket. On Monday I collected in that lot and the same car was at the same meter. Later in the afternoon, I wrote a couple more tickets, eight in all. Tuesday the car was gone. Wednesday the gal that owned the car came in and demanded a court date. In about a week I had to appear as the only witness. The City attorney laid out the charges against the lady. Her attorney questioned why I gave her so many tickets. I told the court that she had parked five days at a 2-hour meter.

Her lawyer tried to discredit me for writing so many tickets. I told him "she is lucky we didn't just tow it away." He got upset with me and tried to make me out as a guy who likes to write tickets. I told him she could have gotten five or six more, but I didn't have time. This made him angry and Judge Gilbert told him to sit down. She asked why this gal had parked five days at a 2-hour meter. The gal didn't want to answer but the Judge said, "I want to know." The gal confessed she had gone to New York City with her boyfriend. The Judge shook her head, smiled slightly and said, "You're guilty, $200.00 fine, pay all tickets at once and don't do that ever again." The girl and her red Mustang disappeared forever.

Good riddance.

The 1980s

(Newspaper Article)

'Goodwill ambassador'

He did more than empty parking meters

By Karen Hermes Smith, staff writer

Birmingham's "goodwill ambassador" and "unofficial mayor" will retire January 4.

Jack Fawcett, the man who repairs and collects the money from the city's 1,300 meters, is trading his 35-year job for a fishing pole and a handful of pinochle cards.

"Birmingham will never be the same without Jack," said Art Lake, president of the Birmingham- Bloomfield

Chamber of Commerce.

"I have for years referred to him as the unofficial mayor — he's so good for the town."

Birmingham shoppers have depended on Fawcett to direct them to stores and retrieve car keys from inside locked cars.

Birmingham merchants shoot the breeze with Fawcett who drops into their stores while making his rounds to tell "stories" (off-color jokes) and gossip.

"He's one of the best PR (public relations) people in the city," said former Police Chief Jerry Tobin, who calls Fawcett "Birmingham's goodwill ambassador."

"He's always the same," said Keith Ege of The Barber Pole on Woodward. "I've never seen Jack when he hasn't got a smile. I think the whole town will miss Jack — there's not many people around like that."

"His smiling face will be definitely missed in downtown Birmingham," said Police Chief Edward Ostin.

Fawcett, 62, was hired by the City on March 1, 1947, to work as a water meter reader.

Friend Ralph Hemmerly, then a water department foreman and now superintendent, asked Fawcett if he wanted a job when Hemmerly dropped over one evening to show off the engagement ring he bought for his fiancee.

Without even asking about the job, Fawcett said yes. "I was tired of working the factory (Pontiac Motor) and wanted to get out of it."

His wife, Shirley, already worked for Birmingham, so it was convenient, Fawcett said. The couple needed only one car.

Eleven years later, the parking meter superintendent's position opened up. Fawcett knew how to do the job — he had filled in for the former superintendent when he went on vacation — so he was asked to take it.

Since 1947, Fawcett estimates he's collected $2.5 million from the meters for the city.

In the process, he's worn out four sets of tires on his collection cart, four pairs of shoes a year and "umpteen" pairs of gloves during the winter time.

During his tenure, the number of meters has grown from 300 to 1,300, and the price of parking from 2 1/2 ¢ to 25 ¢ an hour and the size of Birmingham from a small town to 10 times its former size, Fawcett said.

In the 10 years he's been authorized to write

parking tickets, Fawcett calculates he's written 30,000. "And he hasn't made an enemy out of one of them," Tobin said.

Fawcett said he never picks on one individual and he's always careful to explain to a violator why he's getting a ticket.

Fawcett will miss the people he sees everyday, but not the month of February, he said.

"I can tolerate January, but by the time it gets to February, it seems like winter's going on forever."

Kresge's will probably miss him, Fawcett said. "It'll probably go out of business because of all the doughnuts and pie I've eaten there over the years."

Fawcett will stop downtown and at City Hall every couple of weeks, he said. "I'll have to keep up on the news and stories."

RADAR

About 2 years before I retired, in 1981, I told Capt. Squire that if he wanted someone to work overtime I would do it. I found that the more money you make in the last five years you work, the more your pension would be. The Captain was assistant to Chief Ostin and he had some odd jobs, like checking people on radar. On some days in the afternoon, I wouldn't collect from the meters so I could do other jobs. I used to take an unmarked car, put the radar outfit in and go to streets where people complained there were speeders. I would write their speed down and if a large number were going too fast, he'd put a cop out there and catch them. I did this quite a few times the last two years I worked. It didn't take an officer off of patrol. I would usually get about one hour of overtime. I would sometimes write their license number down if they were really speeding. Usually it was kids going home from high school. It was quite interesting and often the person in the house that complained of people speeding would come and watch. I would show them how it worked and how fast the kids were going. It really impressed some of them, the women especially as they had never seen how radar works.

RETIREMENT #1

I retired on January 4, 1983, after 36 years working for the city, 25 years as a parking meter supervisor. A few years later, I got a call from Gary Klien, parking meter supervisor in Pontiac. He wanted me to repair meters for him. It sounded pretty good, so I went to see him. He asked me what I would need in payment. I decided to take old meters and parts instead of money. This worked great for me and I rebuilt old meters and sold them. One project he wanted was a parking lot uptown behind some stores. He claimed many workers were getting parking tickets and said they weren't getting the correct amount of time they paid for. I exchanged 10 meters with 10 I had repaired. After checking them I found that someone had put the wrong gears in them. They were 3-hour meters but ran down in about two hours. The whole lot had defective meters so I had to change gears in all of them. This caused me to make many trips to Pontiac. It was a great part time job. Gary was a great guy to work for and with. This work lasted for about five years, when they bought electronic meters.

RETIREMENT #2

In my 25 years as a parking meter supervisor, I estimated that I collected over $3,000,000. Also, I kept track of how many parking tickets I wrote. Would you believe over 30,000 in the last 10 years I worked? During this time I attended meter schools in Ypsilanti, Jackson, Saginaw, Detroit and Covington, Kentucky. I also visited the Park-o-meter factory in Russellville, Arkansas two different times on my own, as I was on vacation near there. I enjoyed my job as parking meter supervisor. The 25 years went fast partly because I met so many nice and interesting people. I still see some of the folks I met 25 or 30 years ago. Some I gave tickets to and they still speak to me (some don't). I still work on meters at home. I buy and sell to individuals. I paint them different colors. I also guarantee them for a year. My wife Shirley also worked for the city. We could go home for lunch each day, as we live about a mile from City Hall. She worked 38 years in engineering and building inspection and I worked 36 years.

LOCK PICKER

One thing I learned how to do on my job as a parking meter man was to help people who locked their keys in their car. I got so good with a coat hanger that I could get in most cars. One that I remember well was on Merrill Street on the south side of Shain Park. A man asked me if I could help him get into his new Lincoln. He had locked the keys inside. He also said that Ford Motor had assured him that no one could get in his car if it was locked. I had had so many of these cases that I kept a coat hanger in a small tree beside parking lot 7. I looked up in the tree, got a coat hanger and proceeded to slip it between the rubber around the top of the window. It opened immediately and the man was amazed. He swore and called Ford Motor a few choice words. He then pulled out a $10.00 bill. I told him to keep it, as I was an employee of the Police Department and this service was free. He thanked me several more times. The only car I couldn't get into was a VW. They were tighter than any car I ever knew. When the cars started not having the knobs to pull up with a coat hanger, I couldn't help them. The Police Department had a tool called a "slim Jim". They sometimes scratched the paint, so they quit doing it, unless it was a real emergency. It happened to my wife and me at the Eastern Market in Detroit.

We had a new Pontiac and you couldn't use a coat hanger. I called AAA and they sent a young guy. He had a "slim Jim" tool and after 20 minutes got our car open. I have always carried an extra key in my wallet ever since and that was 20 years ago.

In several of the parking lots, before the decks were built, there were small trees planted along the brick walls. I would hang coat hangers in these trees so I could help people get in their cars. Once I helped an old guy get in the wrong car. It was the same color as his, but a few cars down the line. Once my car keys opened the door of another Pontiac.

TAILS AFTER THE TALES

MERCHANTS THAT I MET
or Characters That I Have Known

One part of my job that I really liked was the different people I would meet. I got to know many of the shopkeepers. They would come out on the sidewalk and talk to me. I still see people I met 40 years ago. I got to know all the barbers in town, but I never got a haircut on city time. Some fellows I knew did. They said their hair grew on city time, so they got it cut on city time. I guess that's one way of looking at it. The Rolls Royce dealer on South Woodward was the only dealer in the state. One day, as I was collecting in front of their showroom, I noticed a Rolls convertible in the showroom. The top was down and it was a dandy. I asked how much it was. The sales man replied $125,000. I said, can you hold it until next Thursday. He said, sure. The next Thursday as I collected in front, I noticed the car was missing. I asked where it was. It seems a doctor had bought it for his wife for a Christmas present. Good way to spend $125,000.00 + tax.

Once in awhile some merchants just wanted to talk and so did I. I knew a lady who lived on Henrietta Steet. Her teenaged daughter worked at Machus Bakery after school. Once in a while I'd go by about 4:00 and stop to talk to her. I'd always ask if she had any broken cookies. Usually she did, but if no one was looking she would sometimes break one in two. I thought she was great. If she reads this I'm sure she'll remember me. Machus Bakery was the best I've ever known. When I went to old Baldwin High School, if I could scrape up 15¢, I'd head for Machus on my lunch hour to buy an eclair, the best I've ever eaten. In 1937-1938 it was hard to scrape up 15¢ sometimes. I was working for 25¢ per hour on Saturday. You young kids won't believe this. I worked all day on Saturday for $2.00.

One store had an Indian gal from India working there. She came out to see me quite often. After I got to know her quite well, I told her that I had heard that Indian gals wore a red dot on their foreheads to show they were virgins. She smiled and said, "That's a damn lie."

JOB OFFERS

Once, while on vacation in Florida, I visited the parking meter department in Clearwater. After talking to the guys for a while, they tried to hire me. They were shorthanded and in tourist season are really busy. They had a pile of meters to repair and no one knew much about them. I thanked them for the offer and left before I got talked into something. The same thing happened in Chapel Hill, North Carolina. I was parked at a meter and an officer came along. We got to talking and when he found out I could repair meters, he told me his chief was looking for a meter repairman. It is a college town and they get lots of jammed meters everyday. I told him thanks, but I was retired. It looked like a nice town to work in and I've thought about it for several years.

End of my story — almost .

A LITTLE MORE

A couple of things I forgot to tell was that I was called back to the city about 5 years after I had retired. It seems that they had decided to raise the meter rates. This was about 1987 or 1986. Anyway there were about 1200 meters that had to be taken off the post and brought into the workshop in the city hall basement. The inside mechanism was taken out, brought in and taken apart. New gears and other parts were then put in. Then they had to be tested and time put on them to see if they ran okay. This whole operation took about six weeks. The thing that took so long was the testing to make sure the meter gave the right amount of time for the coins that were put in. There were 30 minute meters, 1 hour meters, 2 hour meters, 4 hour meters and 12 hour meters. All had different gears so it took some time to make sure each kind of meter was in the right place. About five years later, in about 1992, I got back from three months in Florida on a Sunday afternoon. At about 8:00 pm the phone rang. It was the Chief of Police. He asked if I could come to see him the next morning. When I came in about 8:30 am, he said, "We are going to raise the meter rates and want you to help us." I said OK, but it will take two weeks to get the parts. He replied that they had the parts and were just waiting for me to get home. It was the first week in April. It took about six weeks again and I enjoyed it very much. Mike Coppins is the fellow who took over when I retired January 3, 1983. He is a great guy to work with and for. He now has over 30 years in working for the city. I recalled that I had worked for the city in the 40's, 50's, 60's, 70's, 80's and 90's. I think this is some kind of a record. If not, it must be close. So far I haven't worked in the 2000's (yet). Shirley hasn't either!

ABOUT THIS BOOK

Much credit must be given to Mark Thomas for getting me to write my memories. He thought it would make a great story. I hope he is not disappointed.

The Birmingham-Bloomfield Eccentric®
NEWS *Plus*

INSIDE:
Editorials, Page **20A**
Points of View, Page **21A**
Page 13A

Memorial planners: Four veterans are spearheading an effort to erect a veterams memorial plaque at Birmingham City Hall this Memorial Day. Working on the project are (from left): Jack Colenso, George Forester, Colin Gowan and Jack Fawcett.

Vets want to honor those who gave their lives.

By Helen Niemiec, Staff Writer

A movement that started two years ago with the recognition given to the men and women who fought in the Persian Gulf War is gaining steam to extend that acclaim in Birmingham to those who died in previous wars.

Birmingham veterans contributed to war efforts and are working to install a memorial plaque so the men who gave their lives won't be forgotten.

Memories are fleeting, especially so when many World War II veterans are now in their 70s and 80s. The contributions made, said organizer

69

Jack Colenso, are part of history, but a part that can be forgotten if all that exists are word-of-mouth stories.

There are plenty of stories behind the names that will be on the plaque.

Bill Lawson, who was killed in Vietnam, was a Birmingham man who might have been forgotten from local records. While he lived and went to school here, he married a woman who lived out of state. When her husband went off to war, she moved back to her parents' home. That out-of-state address became Lawson's official address and, when he was killed in action, his "hometown" was his in-laws' address.

"But we knew him and knew that he should be on this list," said Colenso, who has worked for nearly two years assembling the list.

Helping him are George Forester, Colum "Scotty" Gowan and Jack Fawcett. In addition to being veterans, the men also share an interest in history and have lived most — if not their entire— lives in Birmingham.

They look at the list and it's more than names. It is a record of boys they went to school with at the former Baldwin High School or boys who attended

Seaholm with their children, and they have stories that keep the memories of those fallen war heroes alive.

"There were a lot of tragedies," Colenso said, pointing to the names of Robert and Roy Uhlman.

"They were twins. One died at Pearl Harbor and another died in a battle a few months later."

The group is concerned that someone will be missed from the list and are hoping that anyone who knows of a Birmingham veteran killed in World War II, Korea or Vietnam will call Colenso at 649-6542.

"The research is as complete as it can be at this point," Gowan said.

The group also isn't making a federal case of who is Birmingham and who isn't.

"If they went to school here and they had a Birmingham mailing address, they're in," Fawcett said.

The idea for the plaque came during the days after the Desert Storm conflict ended in Iraq. Colenso saw the welcome the soldiers were getting when they returned and wondered what had been done to remember Birmingham veterans from previous wars. When he found that nothing had been done, he assembled his friends and they got started.

Colenso called the city and the Baldwin Library, discovering that no list of veterans existed. A call to U.S. Congressman Joe Knollenberg's office provided a lead - the names of the people in the War Department who could provide the list of veterans.

Since the list isn't available to individuals, the group called upon City Manager Thomas Markus to send a letter asking for the information to be used for a civic purpose.

While the group was waiting on that, a Baldwin Library employee found a dusty old book in its archives that had been assembled by the Moms' Club during World War II and that listed the names of every local boy who went off to war. Gold stars next to the names indicated soldiers killed in action.

The Birmingham plaque will be slightly different than others, since the local one will not list the deceased veteran's rank or military branch. Doing that would leave some veterans with no designations, since the information was available only for soldiers who entered the services in Detroit.

Those who entered while away at college or who had started jobs outside the area weren't on the list supplied by the federal government.

"It seems a little unusual, but we didn't want to exclude some because of that," Gowan said.

With the assembling of names nearly complete, the men are moving on to the next phase—ordering the plaque, designing a display and fund-raising to pay for the project.

TWO JACKS — Fawcett and Colenso
Plaque is inside the front door of City Hall.
(George Forester, Jack Colenso and Colin
"Scotty" Gowan have passed away)
This is the door I came out of to board the bus
taking me to join the Army in March 1943.

Jack's Poem on Retirement

As I was asked a poem to write
      to read on my retirement night,
I sat right down on City time
      and tried to write about 40 lines.
So not to bore you on this fine night,
      I'll keep it short and kind of light.
I only had a few days to go,
      So had to write fast and not be slow.
Between eight and five it had to be done,
      For to write on City time would be more fun.
For having a party I give much thanks,
      at the top of the list my family and
      friends all rank.
I want to thank you, everyone
      for coming tonight and having some fun.
For what is life without some laughs?
      Without it we'd all be just half fast.
Since I've retired, two swell weeks I've had
      To stay at home is not all bad.
Shirley has a list about three feet long
      To keep me home where I belong.
So for 20 days and 20 nights
      I'll paint and paper to her heart's delight
Then Florida calls and winter winds
      Can stay behind when sunshine begins.
So thanks again for my special night,
      Last one out please turn off the lights.

This is Your Life in Reverse (Written on City time.)

As I try to thank you all,
      I thought I'd also have a ball.
I'd write a poem about a few
      of the employees I've known since I was new.
The one that got me started here
      was a guy named Gene.
He described working conditions
      as peachy and keen.
So I signed on for a temporary hitch.
      Almost 36 years later I'm getting the itch.
Retirement calls, as so many know,
      If I stay any longer I'll be counting my toes.
Big Al and I have drunk many a cup.
      We closed all the drug stores
      but never gave up.
Riley also helped us consume
      many cups of caffeine with plenty of cream.
Bob K. worked with us one summer.
      In and out of manholes can sure be a bummer.
He was nimble and quick all covered with dirt.
      We knew he'd succeed and wear a white shirt.
Harry signed on one day in 1952.
      27 years later he decided he was through.
Mox, the grey fox, arrived in 48
      and left in 69 when the going was great.
Two men he hired were Thomason and Squire
      Like in Mickey Spillane's book, *This Gun is*
      For Hire.

Old Russ has left us to follow the sun.
  All the valves he installed are refusing to run.
Big Jim at his age is certainly no dud.
  He loves it when people call him "Old Stud"
Old Charlie is home with Lois all day
  the only thing he can pitch at his age is hay.
Now Nichols is in a class alone
  at parties his poems are seldom out done.
He always gives plungers to his favorite guests
  some don't fit well, but it's all in jest.
Dick Dimock, my boss, can run many a mile
  when he tells jokes, Mike, you better smile.
Bonnie and Jim have learned a way to count
  that is new to me,
They added one and one and ended up with three.
Beau Brummel of course is Ed's other name,
  big cigars and pepsi are really his game.
Brownfield also deserves some cheers
  but he left when he had about 15 years.
Without Millie's help I couldn't retire,
  she figured my pay without raising my ire.
Treasurer office gals are wonderful folks
  to put up with me and my old jokes.
For 24 years and several months plus
  they listened and laughed and
  don't make a fuss.
The cake has been ordered by Inge, I hear
  so let's all eat it with lots of good cheer.
Tortilla Mary is "chicken Mary's" other name,
  chili and refried beans are part of her game.

All the gals in the building sure are keen
      from Ruth to Marge, and Florence,
      the switchboard queen, and all the gals on
      the floors in between.
Steve as Santa is both nimble and quaint,
      When you look at his figure — St. Nick he
      ain't.
This leaves Killeen to pick on I guess
      though his department is hardly ever a mess.
Shirley is staying to keep him in line
      when she'll retire, well, your guess is as
      good as mine.
I've spent half a life time working at City Hall,
      most of the time it has been a real ball.
I've had it made, some friends say about my job,
      and I wouldn't trade places with Ed or with
      Bob.
Many of you have been left out of my lines.
      Please don't feel bad cause your name didn't
      rhyme.
Now as I come to my final line,
      my only wish is that you all enjoy your
      retirement as much as I will enjoy mine.
I've only touched on a few of the friends
      I've met through the years, so to make
      amends
I'll stop right now — though it doesn't rhyme.
          Al, for gosh sakes, cut the cake.
                   Jack Fawcett
                   January 4, 1983

THE MODEL "A" FORD
Article by Jack Fawcett

In 1950 there were nearly a million Model A Ford owners, but hardly any Model A Ford collectors in this country. At this time, most Model As were just 20 year old used cars, reliable and doing a daily job of hauling people to work or for pleasure. Today, all have passed the 70 year old age mark. While a few are still being driven daily, most are in the hands of collectors.

In 1903, Ford introduced his first automobile — the original Model A. After going through much of the alphabet, Ford decided to start a new era with a brand new Model A Ford. On May 26, 1927, the last Model T was built. It was the 15 millionth T and Henry drove it around the plant in Highland Park. The Ford Motor Company had shut down without having plans for a successor. Probably no one but old Henry could get away with something like this. After much hard work and several months later, the Model A was designed for production. On November 1, 1927, production started on the new Model A and was introduced on December 2nd of the same year. It was met with spectacular excitement the world over. It was estimated that over 10 million people saw the new car in the first two days. In two weeks the dealers had orders for 400,000 new cars and on introduction day, production was 100 units a day. Henry announced that by January 1, 1928, production would be 1,000 cars a day. But things didn't improve very fast, as a thorough overhaul had to be made in 34 assembly plants in the USA and Canada. Also, there were 12 overseas plants, as well as independent suppliers. After months of working out various problems in the late months of 1928, the daily output surpassed 6,000 cars a day. The total for 1928 was only 788,000, which was far below expectations. On June 26, 1929, production reached 9,100 cars and trucks per day. This was the highest single day production in automobile history. Ford continued this pace for the remainder of 1929 and finished the year with 1,851,000 cars and trucks. This was 34% of a 5,000,000 car/truck year.

The popularity of the new Model A Ford out produced the nearest competition by 400,000 units. Ford had now reestablished itself as a leader in automobile production.

I became interested in the Model A Ford in 1928 when I was 8 years old. My Grandmother had bought a 1928, four door Model A, and my cousin, who was 14, taught me to drive it. My dad had a 1928 truck to drive where he worked and by the age of 10, I was driving it in the orchard and fields. Once I drove through a 6 foot board fence. However, I didn't buy my own Model A until July, 1972. The 1931 Ford Victoria which is kind of rare. There were only 33,000 produced in 1931 and very few are left.

I bought my A in 1972 and have only driven it around Birmingham and in the yearly parade. It was appraised at $10,000.00.

I found this 1931 Victoria with help from a friend of mine, Ed Francis, who helped write the book, *The Model A as Henry Built It*. My car was re-built by a Ford engineer and I purchased it from him. It runs very good and I once had it up to 60 m.p.h.. With mechanical brakes, you would have to throw out the anchor to stop in a block at this speed.

Old Henry was a genius but also a little eccentric. In the 1900s, while buying motors from the Dodge Bros. for his Model Ts, he ordered the motors to be boxed a certain way to be shipped to his assembly plants. The boards had to be a certain kind of wood, a certain length and width, with holes drilled in certain places. The Dodge Bros. just chalked it up to one of old Henry's goofy ideas. But what they didn't know was that he was using these wood boxes for floor boards in the Model Ts, thus saving millions of dollars per year.

There are many books written about old Henry, but the one I like best is, *We Never Called Him Henry* by Harry H. Bennett. I also like *Henry Ford the Last Billionaire* by William Richards.

What I have given you here is a very brief story of the Model A Ford.

The biggest thing I've done to my Model A is to have a new transmission and clutch. Also, I got four tires and tubes, which I put on myself.

Newspaper Clippings

SHIVER WHILE YOU WORK

Baby it's cold outside. *Just ask Jack Fawcett. He has worked for the City of Birmingham for nearly 30 years. Part of his job is handling cold and ice-coated parking meters. Pulling a "bank" on wheels, Fawcett empties the pennies, dimes and quarters left by thousands of shoppers in the downtown area.*

This meter is in front of Hughes & Hatchers store. The snow was very deep that year 1971.

Mayor William B. Sanders gives Jack his 25 year watch in March, 1972. Bob Kenning, City Manager, on right. Bill Killeen, City Engineer, in middle.

1955 — The DPW boys repair a water main break at the north east corner of Poppleton and Rivenoak Streets. (From left) Pat Shannon, Al Foote in hole, Jack Fawcett and Ralph Hemmerly.

OTHER NEWS STORIES

Raising the Flag

The residents at the Baldwin House in Birmingham observe a solemn moment as the flag is raised Tuesday morning. This flag was special, as it flew over the U.S. Capitol in Washington, D.C. It was presented to the residents by Rep. Joe Knollenberg (third from right). "It's the country's flag, but it belongs to all of you," Knollenberg said.

Jack is second from the right.

═══════ *EPILOGUE* ═══════

Sunday, October 9, 2005

ARTICLE — BIRMINGHAM ECCENTRIC

Time runs out for individual parking meters

by Rebecca Jones, Staff writer

The days of catching a break on someone else's dime at some downtown Birmingham parking meters are over.

Beginning Monday, meters along a portion of old Woodward and Pierce will be replaced with a new "pay and display" parking system.

Instead of feeding meters, drivers will buy time-stamped tickets at one of six central parking stands and affix the receipt inside the driver's window.

The system is set for a 90-day trial along old Woodward between Maple and Merrill and the west side of Pierce between Martin and Merrill.

It is just one of the changes the city is considering instead of traditional parking meters, said Ellen DeView, staff and services coordinator for Birmingham police.

October 12, 2005

Birmingham-Bloomfield EAGLE

Time's up for parking meters

*Experimental program may allow debit
and credit for parking.*

By Christina Ulaj, Staff Writer

Meters may be a thing of the past as the city experiments with its current parking system.

The City of Birmingham was negotiating the purchase of 350 meter mechanisms to place throughout the city when City Manager Tom Markus suggested holding off on the purchases and experimenting with types of technology.

Park and Display is a parking system that would eliminate meters altogether. Each unit will take the place of about eight to ten meters, and units will be spaced out down the streets. People can park their vehicles, walk over to the system, insert their method of payment, take a receipt, place the receipt on the dash, and return to purchase more time if they want. The systems allows people to pay with quarters, credit cards or debit cards.

Index

Parking for a Nickel

Businesses, Corporations & Other Law Abiding Institutions

Weir Manuel Realtors ©
Since 1950
In the Heart of Downtown Birmingham

Jack, we miss your smiling face whenever we hear the coins rattle down the gooseneck into the coin cart from the meters in front of our office.

2215 COLE STREET, BIRMINGHAM, MI 48009

248 644 1900   248 644 1911

INFO@SWANSONMEADSARCHITECTS.NET

The woman-owned architecture firm of Glenda Meads, AIA and Karen Swanson, AIA, established in 1999 in downtown Birmingham, is proud to announce their recent relocation to the Birmingham Rail District. Our firm has been dedicated to a high quality commercial and residential built environment for Birmingham. The energy of similar business committed to a Rail District revitalization makes this a vibrant home for us.

Birmingham Historical Museum
556 West Maple Road
Birmingham, Michigan

Thank you, Jack Fawcett. The mission of the Birmingham Historical Society is to promote knowledge of the history of Birmingham, Michigan area by collecting and preserving records which help explain and interpret our past. Parking For A Nickel is a valuable contribution towards fulfilling our mission.

90

Friends, Co-workers and People Jack Ticketed

Great work, Jack
> Pam & Mark Thomas

Thank you, Jack, for all your years of service to the citizens of Birmingham.
> Bob & Coco Siewert

Thanks for preserving the history, facts, and foibles of our city.
> Diane K. Bert, Ph.D.
> Vice President, Birmingham Historical Society

To Jack being one of the most cheerful and friendly servants in our town. Thanks.
> Marguerite Hague

Best wishes from new friends and admirers.
> Hazel Proctor & Jay Carp

Jack, thanks for saving me from the Baldwin boys room smoker, in 1937.
> Max

You gave me 42 tickets you *#@%#*%*
> Anonymous acquaintance

Thanks for your contribution to the Birminham Historical Society.
> Fred & Judy Amrose

Jack, the Board appreciates your contribution of the proceeds from this book to the Historical Society.
> John A. Bluth

More Friends, Co-workers and People Jack Ticketed

Make history yours, Jack.
> Gould-McElhone Family

Thanks for your many years of service to this city and the Birmingham Kiwanis Club.
> Your many friends in Kiwanis

Parking For a Nickel is a wonderful collection of stories and your donation to the Historical Society is very generous. Thank you.
> Don Robinson

Congratulates Jack Fawcett on the publication of this book, which through its 'stories of the parking meter', chronicles the life of a town whose owes it existence to the rise of the automobile and whose efforts to balance the place of the automobile and the qualities of a liveable city make it the vibrant community it remains.
> Swanson Meads Architecture

You were the best ever for collecting money, Jack. Thanks and best wishes.
> The Guys & Dolls at City Hall